PUBLISHIG HOUSE
KULTURE KITCHEN

POWER XL
AIR FRYER GRILL
COOKBOOK

The Cookbook Series That Will Help You To Conquer Your New Favorite Kitchen Appliance!

Snack & Sandwich Vol.1

POWER XL
AIR FRYER GRILL
COOKBOOK

EVERYDAY QUICK & EASY RECIPES FOR AIR FRYER LOVERS

PUBLISHIG HOUSE
KULTURE KITCHEN

© 2021 Kulture Kitchen Publishing House - All rights reserved.

Photography Humbert Castillo
Graphic design Yuka Okuma
Editorial coordination Lizzie Martin

First edition March 2021

The following book is reproduced below to provide information that is as accurate and reliable as possible. Regardless, purchasing this book can be seen as consent because both the publisher and the author of this book are in no way experts on the topics discussed within. Any recommendations or suggestions that are made herein are for entertainment purposes only. Professionals should be consulted as needed before undertaking any of the actions endorsed herein. This declaration is deemed fair and valid by both the American Bar Association and the Committee of Publishers Association and is legally binding throughout the United States. Furthermore, the transmission, duplication, or reproduction of any of the following work, including specific information, will be considered an illegal act irrespective of if it is done electronically or in print. This extends to creating a secondary or tertiary copy of the work or a recorded document and can only express written consent from the publisher. All additional rights reserved. The information in the following pages is broadly considered a truthful and accurate account of facts. As such, any inattention, use, or misuse of the information in question by the reader will render any resulting actions solely under their purview. There are no scenarios in which the publisher or the original author of this work can be in any fashion deemed liable for any hardship or damages that may befall them after undertaking the information described herein. Additionally, the following pages' information is intended only for informational purposes and should thus be thought of as universal. As befitting its nature, it is presented without assurance regarding its prolonged validity or interim quality. Trademarks that are mentioned are done without written consent and can in no way be considered an endorsement from the trademark holder.

Table of Content

INTRODUCTION — 7

SNACK & SANDWICH — 9

- Prosciutto-Wrapped Parmesan Asparagus — 11
- Bacon-Wrapped Jalapeño Poppers — 13
- Spicy Buffalo Chicken Dip — 15
- Bacon Jalapeño Cheese Bread — 17
- Bacon Cheeseburger Dip — 19
- Pork Rind Tortillas — 21
- Mozzarella Sticks — 23
- Bacon-Wrapped Onion Rings — 25
- Mini Sweet Pepper Poppers — 27
- Spicy Spinach Artichoke Dip — 29
- Garlic Cheese Bread — 31
- Loaded Roasted Broccoli — 33
- Sausage-Stuffed Mushroom Caps — 35
- Zucchini Parmesan Chips — 37
- Kale Chips — 39
- Italian Stuffed Sandwich — 41
- Weekend Sandwich — 43
- Peppery Turkey Sandwiches — 45
- Italian Eggplant Sandwich — 47
- Prosciutto Sandwich — 49
- Roasted Bell Pepper Vegetable Salad — 51
- Mushroom, Onion, and Feta Frittata — 53
- Crispy Onion Rings — 55
- Crisp Potato Wedges — 57
- Roasted Heirloom Tomato with Baked Feta — 59
- Garam Masala Beans — 61
- Fried Pickles — 63
- Roasted Eggplant — 65
- Pita-Style Chips — 67
- Flatbread — 69
- Radish Chips — 71
- Calzone — 73
- Hash Brown Toast — 75
- Roasted Garlic — 77
- Spicy Cheese Meatballs — 79
- Egg & Bacon Sandwich — 81
- Ricotta Wraps & Spring Chicken — 83
- Chicken Wrapped in Bacon — 85

Veal Club Sandwich	87
Pork Club Sandwich	89
Parmesan Herb Focaccia	91
Jicama Fries	93
Fried Green Tomatoes	95
Cauliflower Relish	97
Baked Zucchini Fries	99
Homemade Tater Tots	101

Introduction

Elsie Tyler is a passionate cookbook writer with over a decade of culinary expertise. Known for her culinary skills and high standard, she has combined her classic recipes tailored to use with the modern cooking appliance in her new cookbook series "The Complete Power XL Air Fryer Grill Cookbook" Kulture Kitchen Publishing House. She loves to employ innovations in cooking by keeping the traditional elements and richness.

We can always find the art of simplicity in her recipes, making her a step ahead of many innovative cooking methods. All of her books include self-tested recipes, and the pleasure of sharing exciting experiments is evident in most of her recipe works.

Popularly known as a 'wizard of recipe developer' among her circle, she contributes recipes to several reputed magazines. She helps you discover something new and impressive. Beyond her books, she maintains a strong influence among her friends and family as an enthusiast of healthy eating and living.

Having spent considerable time writing the series "The Complete Power XL Air Fryer Grill Cookbook", she has carefully penned her research with super versatile meal ideas without compromising quality and nutritional values. Her approach to modern food tech is mind-blowing.

This Cookbook Series is a pioneering endeavor blended with modern cooking with traditional values by focusing on healthy, balanced food. It is a reference series for people who love having healthy food.

Snack & Sandwich

Prosciutto-Wrapped Parmesan Asparagus

Ready in about 20 min | Servings 4 | Normal

Ingredients:

- 1-pound of asparagus
- 12 (0.5-ounce) slices of prosciutto
- 1 tablespoon of coconut oil, melted
- 2 teaspoons of lemon juice
- 1/8 teaspoon of red pepper flakes
- 1/3 cup of grated Parmesan cheese
- 2 tablespoons of salted butter, melted

Directions:

1. Place an asparagus spear onto a slice of prosciutto on a clean work surface.

2. Drizzle with the lemon juice and coconut oil. Sprinkle over asparagus with red pepper flakes and Parmesan. Roll prosciutto with a spear of asparagus. Put the basket into the Power Xl Air Fryer.

3. Select bake mode the set the temperature to 375° F and set the timer for a further 10 minutes.

4. Before eating, sprinkle asparagus roll with butter.

Bacon-Wrapped Jalapeño Poppers

Ready in about 27 min | Servings 4 | Normal

Ingredients:

- 6 jalapeños (about 4" long each)
- 3-ounces of full-Fat: cream cheese
- 1/3 cup of shredded medium Cheddar cheese
- 1/4 teaspoon of garlic powder
- 12 slices sugar-free bacon

Directions:

1. Cut the tops off the jalapeños and slice lengthwise in two sections down the middle. Use a knife to cut the white membrane and pepper seeds with caution.

2. Place the cream cheese, Cheddar, and garlic powder in a large microwave-safe dish. Microwave, then stir for 30 seconds. Mixture the spoon of cheese with the jalapeños.

3. Wrap a strip of bacon around half of each jalapeño, shielding the pepper entirely. Put the basket into the Power XL Air Fryer.

4. Select bake mode the set the temperature to 400° F and change the timer for 12 minutes.

5. When the timer reaches 0, then press the cancel button

6. Switch the peppers halfway through the cycle of preparation. Serve warm.

Spicy Buffalo Chicken Dip

Ready in about 20 min | Servings 4 | Easy

Ingredients:

- 1 cup of cooked, diced chicken breast
- 8 ounces of full-Fat: cream cheese, softened
- 1/2 cup of buffalo sauce
- 1/3 cup of full-Fat: ranch dressing
- 1/3 cup of chopped pickled jalapeños
- 1 ½ cups of shredded medium Cheddar cheese, divided
- 2 scallions, sliced

Directions:

1. Place chicken into a large bowl. Add cream cheese, buffalo sauce, and ranch dressing. Stir until thespices are well mixed and mostly smooth. Fold in jalapeños and 1 cup Cheddar.

2. Pour the mixture into a 4-cup round baking dish andplace the remaining Cheddar on top. Place the dish into the Power XL Air Fryer basket.

3. Adjust the temperature to 350°F and set the timer for 10 minutes.

4. When setting a cooking time less than 20 minutes, first set the cooking time to 20 minutes.

Then, turn the time/darkness control knob to the desired cooking time

5. When done, the top will be brown and bubbling. Top with sliced scallions. Serve warm.

Bacon Jalapeño Cheese Bread

Ready in about 25 min | Servings 2 | Yields 8 sticks | Normal

Ingredients:

- 2 cups of shredded mozzarella cheese
- ¼ cup of grated Parmesan cheese
- ¼ cup of chopped pickled jalapeños
- 2 large eggs
- 4 slices of sugar-free bacon, cooked and chopped

Directions:

1. Mix all ingredients in a large bowl. Cut a piece of parchment to fit your Power XL Air Fryer basket.

2. Dampen your hands with a bit of water and press out the mixture into a circle. You may need to separate this into two smaller cheese bread, depending on your fryer's size.

3. Place the parchment and cheese bread into the AirFryer basket.

4. Adjust the temperature to 320°F and set the timer for 15 minutes.

5. Carefully flip the bread when 5 minutes remain.

6. When fully cooked, the top will be golden brown. Serve warm and enjoy!

Bacon Cheeseburger Dip

Ready in about 30 min | Servings 6 | Normal

Ingredients:

- 8 ounces of full-Fat: cream cheese
- 1/4 cup of full-Fat: mayonnaise
- 1/4 cup of full-Fat: sour cream
- 1/4 cup of chopped onion
- 1 teaspoon of garlic powder
- 1 tablespoon of Worcestershire sauce 1
- 1/4 cups of shredded medium Cheddar cheese, divided
- ½-pound of cooked 80/20 ground beef
- 6 slices of sugar-free bacon, cooked and crumbled
- 2 large of pickle spears, chopped.

Directions:

1. In a large microwave-safe bowl, place the cream cheese and microwave for 45 seconds. Stir in mayonnaise, sour cream, onion, powdered garlic, and one cup of Worcestershire Cheddar sauce. Add the bacon and the ground beef. Sprinkle over leftover Cheddar.

2. Place the bowl in 6 " and put it in the basket of the Power XL Air Fryer.

3. Select bake mode the set the temperature to 400° F and adjust the timer for 10 minutes.

4. When the top is golden, bubbling sprinkles the pickles over the dish and serves warm.

Pork Rind Tortillas

Ready in about 15 min | Servings 4 | Yields 4 tortillas| Easy

Ingredients:

- 1-ounce of pork rinds
- 3/4 cup of shredded mozzarella cheese
- 2 tablespoons of full-Fat: cream cheese
- 1 large egg

Directions:

1. Install pork rinds in a food processor and pulse until finely soiled.

2. Place the mozzarella in a large, safe microwave bowl. Break-in small pieces of the cream cheese and add to the bowl. Microwave for 30 seconds, or until both kinds of cheese are melted and easily stirred into a ball. To the cheese mixture, add the ground pork rinds and the egg.

3. Continue to stir till the mixture forms a ball. If it cools too much and hardens the cheese, then microwave for another 10 seconds.

4. Set the dough aside into four small balls. Place each dough ball between two parchment sheets, and roll into a 1/4 flat layer.

5. Place tortillas in a single layer Power XL Air Fryer basket; work in batches where necessary.

6. Set the temperature to 400° F and adjust the timer for 5 minutes.

7. When fully cooked, the tortillas will become crispy and firm. Serve immediately and enjoy!

Mozzarella Sticks

Ready in about 1 hour 10 min | Servings 3 | Yields 12 sticks | Normal

Ingredients:

- 6 (1-ounce) mozzarella string cheese sticks
- 1/2 cup of grated Parmesan cheese
- ½- an ounce of pork rinds, finely ground
- 1 teaspoon of dried parsley
- 2 large eggs

Directions:

1. Put the sticks of mozzarella on a cutting board and cut in half. Freeze to stand for 45 minutes or until solid. When freezing overnight, cut frozen sticks after 1 hour and put them in an airtight zip-top storage bag for future use.

2. Combine the Parmesan, ground pork rinds, and parsley in a large bowl.

3. Then whisk eggs in a medium bowl.

4. Brush a frozen mozzarella over beaten eggs, then coat in a Parmesan sauce. Repeat for unused sticks. Place the mozzarella sticks in the bowl of the Power XL Air Fryer.

5. Adjust the temperature to 400° F and set the timer to golden for 10 minutes.

6. Serve hot and enjoy!

Bacon-Wrapped Onion Rings

Ready in about 15 min | Servings 4 | Normal

Ingredients:

- 1 large onion, peeled
- 1 tablespoon of sriracha
- 8 slices of sugar-free bacon

Directions:

1. Slice of the ointment into 1/4"-thick slices. Take two slices of onion and tie the bacon around the rings. Repeat for the remaining onion and bacon.

2. Select bake mode the set the temperature to 350° F and change the timer for 10 minutes.

3. Use pliers to rotate the onion rings halfway through the cooking time. Bacon will be crispy when fully fried. Eat hot and enjoy it!

Mini Sweet Pepper Poppers

Ready in about 30 min | Servings 4 | Yields 16 halves| Normal

Ingredients:

- 8 mini sweet peppers
- 4 ounces of full-Fat: cream cheese, softened
- 4 slices of sugar-free bacon, cooked and crumbled
- 1/4 cup of shredded pepper jack cheese

Directions:

1. Cut the pepper tops and slice on half lengthwise each. To cut seeds and membranes using a small knife.
2. Put together the cream cheese, bacon, and pepper jack in a shallow tub.
3. In each sweet pepper, put 3 teaspoons of the mixture and press smoothly hard—place in basket fryer.
4. Select bake mode the set the temperature to 400° F, and set the timer for eight minutes.
5. When the timer reaches 0, then press the cancel button
6. Serve sweet and enjoy!

Spicy Spinach Artichoke Dip

Ready in about 20 min | Servings 6 | Easy

Ingredients:

- 10 ounces of frozen spinach, drained and thawed
- 1 (14-ounce) can of artichoke hearts, drained and chopped
- 1/4 cup of chopped pickled jalapeños
- 8 ounces of full-Fat: cream cheese, softened
- 1/4 cup of full-Fat: mayonnaise
- 1/4 cup of full-Fat: sour cream
- 1/2 teaspoon of garlic powder
- ¼ cup of grated Parmesan cheese
- 1 cup of shredded pepper jack cheese

Directions:

1. Combine the ingredients in a 4-cup baking dish. Put the basket into the Power XL Air Fryer.
2. Select bake mode the set the temperature to 320° F and change the timer for 10 minutes.
3. When the timer reaches 0, then press the cancel button
4. Start as orange, then bubble. Serve fresh and enjoy!

Garlic Cheese Bread

Ready in about 20 min | Servings 2 | Easy

Ingredients:

- 1 cup of shredded mozzarella cheese
- 1/4 cup of grated Parmesan cheese
- 1 large egg
- 1/2 teaspoon of garlic powder

Directions:

1. Mix the ingredients in a large bowl. Cut a piece of parchment to fit your basket with Power XL Air Fryer. Press the mixture on the parchment in a circle, and place it in the basket of the Air Fryer.

2. Select bake mode the set the temperature to 350° F and change the timer for 10 minutes.

3. When the timer reaches 0, then press the cancel button

4. Serve hot and enjoy!

Loaded Roasted Broccoli

Ready in about 20 min | Servings 2 | Easy

Ingredients:

- 3 cups of fresh broccoli florets
- 1 tablespoon of coconut oil
- 1/2 cup of shredded sharp Cheddar cheese
- 1/4 cup of full-Fat: sour cream
- 4slices of sugar-free bacon, cooked and crumbled
- 1 scallion, sliced

Directions:

1. Bring the broccoli into the Power XL Air Fryer tank and drizzle it with coconut oil.

2. Select bake mode the set the temperature to 350° F and change the timer 10 minutes longer.

3. Toss a basket for two or three times during the training or avoid burning spots.

4. Remove from the fryer as the broccoli continues to crisp at the top. Cover to garnish with melted cheese, sour cream, and crumbled slices of bacon and scallion.

Sausage-Stuffed Mushroom Caps

Ready in about 16 min | Servings 2 | Easy

Ingredients:

- 6 large portobello mushroom caps
- ½-pound of Italian sausage
- 1/4 cup of chopped onion
- 2 tablespoons of blanched finely ground almond flour
- ¼ cup of grated Parmesan cheese
- 1 teaspoon of minced fresh garlic

Directions:

1. Use a spoon to hollow each cap of the mushrooms, and save scrapings.

2. Brown the sausage in a medium saucepan over medium heat for around 10 minutes, or until fully cooked and no pink remains. Drain and then apply stored scrapings of mushroom, cabbage, almond flour, parmesan, and garlic. Fold ingredients gently together and continue cooking for a further minute, then remove from fire.

3. Scoop the mixture uniformly into mushroom caps and place the caps in a 6 round tub. Put the pan in the basket for the Power XL Air Fryer.

4. Select bake mode the set the temperature to 375° F, and set the timer for 8 minutes.

5. The tops will be browned and bubbling when done frying, and serve soft.

Zucchini Parmesan Chips

Ready in about 20 min | Servings 1 | Easy

Ingredients:

- 2 medium zucchinis
- 1-ounceof pork rinds
- 1/2 cup of grated Parmesan cheese
- 1 large egg

Directions:

1. Slice of zucchini in 1/4"-thick strips. Put 30 minutes between two layers of paper towels or a clean kitchen towel to eliminate any extra moisture.
2. Put pork rinds in a food processor and pulse until finely ground. Pour into a medium bowl and combine it with Parmesan.
3. Beat the egg in a shallow saucepan.
4. Dip the zucchini slices in the egg mixture and then in the pork rind mixture, cover as thoroughly as possible. Put each slice carefully in a single layer of the Power XL Air Fryer bowl, operating as required in batches.
5. Change the temperature to 320° F and set a 10-minute timer.
6. Flip chips halfway into time to cook. Serve hot and enjoy!

Kale Chips

Ready in about 10 min | Servings 4 | Easy

Ingredients:

- 4 cups of steamed kale
- 2 teaspoons of avocado oil
- 1/2 teaspoon of salt

Directions:

1. Swirl kale in avocado oil in a large tub, and sprinkle with salt. Place it in the basket of Power XL Air Fryer.

2. Change the temperature to 400° f and set a 5-minute timer.

3. When setting a cooking time less than 20 minutes, first set the cooking time to 20 minutes.

Then, turn the time/darkness control knob to the desired cooking time

4. When finished, the kale would be crispy. Serve forthwith.

Italian Stuffed Sandwich

Ready about in: 1 hr and 10 min|Serves 2|Easy

Ingredients

- ½ kg of flour medium strength.
- 10gr of fresh yeast
- 230 - 240ml of water.
- 60gr butter or oil.
- 1 teaspoon salt
- 1 teaspoon of sugar

Directions:

To do it manually: Dissolve the yeast in a little warm water.

Place the flour in the shape of a volcano in a large container. In the center place the oil, sugar, and salt. Move with a wooden spoon. Add the yeast and begin to integrate from the inside out. Now integrated, pass them to the work table.

Knead until a homogeneous mass is observed. It should not be stuck in the hands. Cover and let stand, about 1 hour.

Then spread the dough, trying to have a thickness of 2 to 6 millimeters. Cut small rectangles and measure the center.

Place filling in the lower center part. Spread a little water on the edges with a thin brush to seal.

Cut the excess if you do it by machine, proceed according to the instructions. Place in the Power XL Air Fryer for 10 - 12 minutes at 380° F.

They a Reserved up with creams to taste.

Weekend Sandwich

Ingredients

- 12 slices Sandwich bread
- 12 slices of turkey ham
- 6 slices of vegan cheese
- 1½ cups of grated yellow cheese
- 1 cup of milk cream
- 100 g of Butter
- Salt and pepper to taste

Directions:

First, spread a little butter on the bread slices. Place one of the loaves, two slices of ham, one of cheese and close.

Place in the Power XL Air Fryer and fry at 150°C for 2 minutes.

Meanwhile, in a bowl, mix the cheese, cream, salt, and pepper. Cover the sandwich with the mixture. Fry at 170°C for 4 minutes until golden brown.

Peppery Turkey Sandwiches

Read about in: 15 min| Servings: 4

Ingredients

- 7 ounces thinly sliced cracked black pepper-seasoned turkey breast
- 4 (3/4-ounce) slices Monterey Jack cheese with jalapeño peppers
- 3 (1-ounce) slices multigrain bread
- 4 tablespoons creamy mustard blend
- ½ cup mild banana pepper rings, drained

Directions:

Preheat broiler to your Power XL Air Fryer

Place bread slices on a baking sheet.

Toast bread on both sides

Spread 2 tablespoon mustard blend over each bread slice.

Arrange 2 ounces turkey on each bread slice. Place banana pepper rings evenly over turkey; top sandwiches with cheese slices.

Broil 5 minute or until cheese melts

Enjoy

Italian Eggplant Sandwich

Ready in about 26 min | Servings 2 | Easy

Ingredients:

- 1 eggplant, sliced
- 2 teaspoons of parsley, dried
- Salt and black pepper to the taste
- ½ cup of breadcrumbs
- ½ teaspoon of Italian seasoning
- ½ teaspoon of garlic powder
- ½ teaspoon of onion powder
- 2 tablespoons of milk
- 4 bread slices
- Cooking spray
- ½ cup of mayonnaise
- ¾ cup of tomato sauce
- 2 cups of mozzarella cheese, grated

Directions:

1. Season eggplant slices with salt and pepper, leave aside for 10minutes and then pat dry them well.
2. In a bowl, mix parsley with breadcrumbs, Italian seasoning, onionand garlic powder, salt and black pepper, and stir.
3. In another bowl, mix milk with mayo and whisk well.
4. Brush eggplant slices with mayo mix, dip them in breadcrumbs,place them in your Power XL Air Fryer's basket, spray with cooking oil andcook them at 400° F for 15 flipping them after 8minutes.
5. Brush each bread slice with olive oil and arrange 2 on a workingsurface.

6. Add mozzarella and parmesan on each, add baked eggplant slices, spread tomato sauce and basil, and top with the other bread slices, greased side down.

7. Divide sandwiches between plates, cut them in halves, and serve for lunch. Enjoy!

Prosciutto Sandwich

Ready in about 15 min | Servings 1 | Normal

Ingredients:

- 2 bread slices
- 2 mozzarella slices
- 2 tomato slices
- 2 prosciutto slices
- 2 basil leaves
- 1 teaspoon of olive oil
- A pinch of salt and black pepper

Directions:

1. Arrange mozzarella and prosciutto on a bread slice.

2. Season with salt and pepper, place in your Power XL Air Fryer and cook at 400° F for 5 minutes.

3. Drizzle oil over prosciutto, add tomato and basil, cover with the otherbread slice, cut the sandwich in half and serve.

Enjoy!

Roasted Bell Pepper Vegetable Salad

Ready in about 35 min | Servings 4 | Normal

Ingredients:

- 1½ ounces of yogurt
- 1 medium-sized red bell pepper
- 2ounces of rocket leaves
- 3 teaspoons of lime juice
- 1 romaine lettuce
- 1 ounce of olive oil
- Ground black pepper and salt to taste

Directions:

1. Heat your power XL Air Fryer to 392°F and place the bell pepper into it. Roast for 10 minutes until a bit charred. Put the pepper in a bowl, cover, and leave for about 15minutes.

2. When the timer reaches 0, then press the cancel button

3. Divide the bell pepper into 4, remove skin and seeds and then slice the pepper into thin strips.

4. Mix the lime juice, olive oil, and yogurt thoroughly together in a bowl. Add the salt and pepper as required and stir.

5. Add the rocket leaves, lettuce, and pepper strips into the yogurt mixtureand toss to mix.

Mushroom, Onion, and Feta Frittata

Ready in about 40 min | Servings 4 | Normal

Ingredients:

- 4 cups of button mushrooms, cleaned and cut thinly into ¼ inch
- 6eggs
- 1 red onion, peeled and sliced thinly into ¼ an inch
- 6 tablespoons of feta cheese, crumbled
- 2 tablespoons of olive oil
- 1 pinch of salt

Directions:

1. Add olive oil to a sauté pan and swirl the onions and mushrooms around under medium heat until tender. Remove from heatand cool on a dry kitchen towel.

2. Select bake mode the set the temperature to preheat Power XL Air Fryer to 330°F. Whisk the eggs thoroughly in a mixing bowland add a pinch of salt.

3. Coat the inside and bottom of an 8-in heat resistant baking dish lightly with spray. Pour the whisked eggs into the baking dish, add the onion and mushroom mixture and then add the cheese.

4. Place the dish in the cooking basket and cook 27 to 30 minutes in the Air Fryer or until an inserted knife in the frittata center comes out clean.

Crispy Onion Rings

Ready in about 35 min | Servings 2 | Easy

Ingredients:

- 1 big of sized onion, thinly sliced
- 8 ounces of milk
- 1 egg
- 6 ounces of breadcrumbs
- 1 teaspoon of baking powder
- 10 ounces of flour
- 1 teaspoon of salt

Directions:

1. Heat your Power XL Air Fryer to 360°F for 10 minutes.
2. Detach the onion slices to separate rings.
3. Mix the baking powder, flour, and salt in a bowl.
4. Put the onion rings into the flour mixture to coat them. Beat the egg and the milk and stir into the flour to form a batter. Dip the flour-coated rings in the batter.
5. Put the bread crumbs in a small tray, place the onion rings in it, and ensureall sides are well coated.
6. Place the rings in the fryer basket and airfry for 10 minutes until crisp. Enjoy!

Crisp Potato Wedges

Ready in about 40 min | Servings 4 | Normal

Ingredients:

- 3 teaspoons of olive oil
- 2 big potatoes
- ¼ cup of sweet chili sauce
- ¼ cup of sour cream

Directions:

1. Slice the potatoes lengthwise tocreate a wedge shape.

2. Select bake mode the set the temperature to Power XL Air Fryer to 356°F.

3. Place the wedges in a bowl and add the oil. Toss lightly until the potatoes are fully coated with the oil.

4. Put into the cooking basket with the skin side facing down and cook for about 15 minutes. Toss, then cook for an other 10 minutes until golden brown.

5. Best served while warm with chili source and sour cream.

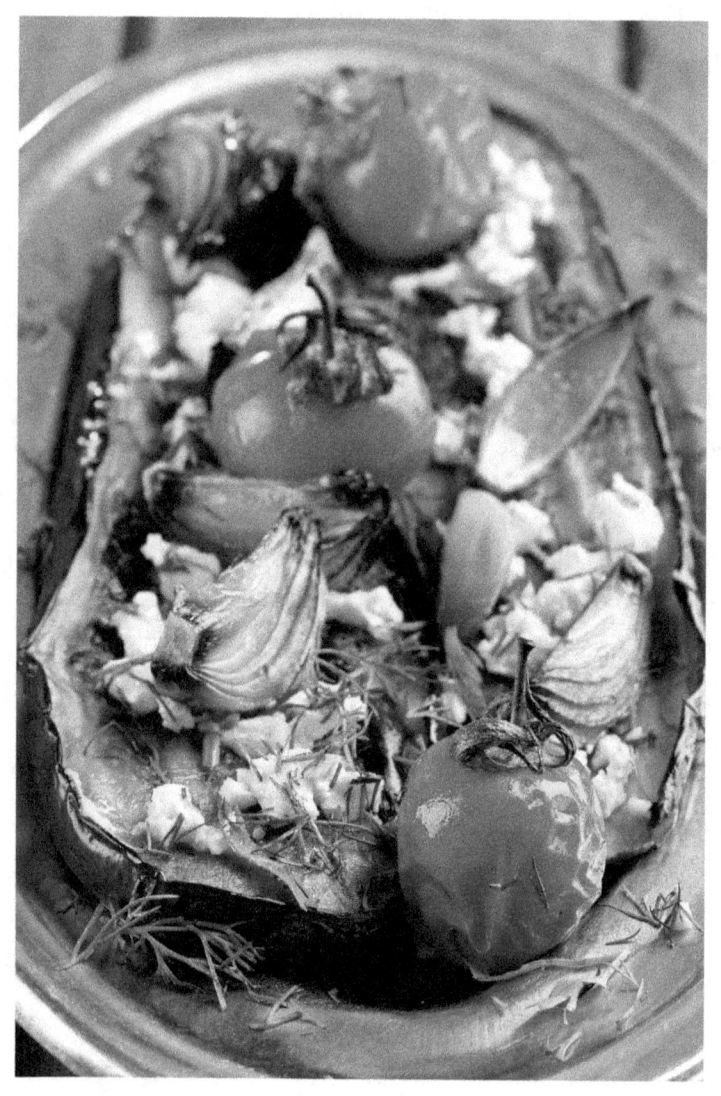

Roasted Heirloom Tomato with Baked Feta

Ready in about 35 min | Servings 4 | Easy

Ingredients:

For the Tomato:

- 2 heirloom tomatoes, sliced thickly into ½ inch circular slices
- 1 8-ounceof feta cheese, sliced thickly into ½ inch circular slices
- ½ cup of red onions, sliced thinly
- 1 pinch of salt
- 1 tablespoon of olive oil

For the Basil Pesto:

- ½ cup of basil, chopped roughly
- ½ cup of parsley, roughly chopped
- 3 tablespoons of pine nuts, toasted
- ½ cup of parmesan cheese, grated
- 1 garlic clove
- 1 pinch of salt
- ½ cup of olive oil

Directions:

1. Begin by making the pesto. To do this, combine garlic, parmesan, parsley, toasted pine nuts, basil, and salt in a food processor.

2. Turn it on and gradually add the olive oil to incorporate into the pesto. Once done, store and put in the refrigerator until ready to use.

3. Preheat the Power XL Air Fryer to 390°F. Pat dry tomato with a paper towel. Spread atablespoon of the pesto on top of each slice of tomato and top with the feta.Add1 tablespoon of olive oil to the red onions and toss; place on top of the feta.

4. Now place the feta / tomatoes into the cooking basket and cook until the feta is brownish and starts to soften or 12 to 14 minutes.

5. Add a pinch of salt and 1 spoonful of basil pesto. Serve and enjoy.

Garam Masala Beans

Ready in about 17 min | Servings 4 | Easy

Ingredients:

- 9-ounce of Beans
- 2 Eggs
- 1/2 cup of breadcrumbs
- 1/2 cup of flour
- 1/2 teaspoon of garam masala
- 2 teaspoon of chili powder
- Olive Oil
- Salt to taste

Directions:

1. Preheat the Power XL Air Fryer at 350°F. Combine chilipowder, garam masala, flour, and salt in a bowl, mixing well. Beat the eggs and set one side.
2. Pour the bread crumbs on a separate plate, then coat the beans with the flour mixture. Now dip beans into the egg mixture and next, into the bread crumbs. Do this with all the beans.
3. Place the beans into the Air Fryer tray and cook for 4 minutes. Open and coat the beans with oil and cook once more for another 3 minutes.

Serve warm and enjoy!

Fried Pickles

Ready in about 15 min | Servings 4 | Easy

Ingredients:

- 1 tablespoon of coconut flour
- 1/3 cup of blanched finely ground almond flour
- 1 teaspoon of chili powder
- 1/4 teaspoon of garlic powder
- 1 large egg
- 1 cup of sliced pickles

Directions:

1. In a medium dish, mix the coconut flour, almond meal, chili powder, and garlic powder.
2. Whisk the egg in a tiny mug.
3. Pat with a paper towel on each pickle and dunk in the egg. Then dredge in the mixture with flour. Put the pickles in the bowl for Power Xl Air Fryer.
4. Switch to 400° F and set the timer for 5 minutes.
5. Flip the pickles halfway through the duration of preparation.

Roasted Eggplant

Ready in about 30 min | Servings 4 | Easy

Ingredients:

- 1 large eggplant
- 2 tablespoons of olive oil
- 1/4 teaspoon of salt
- 1/2 teaspoon of garlic powder

Directions:

1. Cut eggplant top and bottom. Break the eggplant into small thick strips.
2. Spray the slices with the olive oil and sprinkle with salt and garlic powder. Put the pieces of the eggplant in the container of your Power XL Air Fryer.
3 Select bake mode the set the temperature to 390° F and change the timer for 15 minutes.
4. When the timer reaches 0, then press the cancel button
5. Serve forthwith and enjoy!

Pita-Style Chips

Ready in about 15 min | Servings 4 | Easy

Ingredients:

- 1 cup of shredded mozzarella cheese
- ¼ cup of blanched finely ground almond flour
- ½ teaspoon ground black pepper
- ½ teaspoon dried basil
- ½ cup olive oil
- 1 large egg

Directions:

1. Put the mozzarella in a large microwave and microwave bowl for 30 seconds or until it has melted. Add remaining ingredients and stir to a smooth finish; the dough quickly shapes into a ball. Microwave for 15 seconds if the dough is too rough.
2. Roll the dough out into a wide rectangle between two sheets of parchment and then use a knife to cut chips in a triangle shape. Place the chips in the basket for Power XL Air Fryer.
3. Select bake mode the set the temperature to 400° F and set the timer for 5 minutes.
4. When finished, the chips would be golden in color and solid. They'll get much firmer as they cool off.

Flatbread

Ready in about 11 min | Servings 2 | Easy

Ingredients:

- 1 cup of shredded mozzarella cheese
- 1/4 cup of blanched finely ground almond flour
- 1 ounce of full-Fat: cream cheese, softened

Directions:

1. Melt mozzarella in a big, microwave-safe bowl for 30 seconds. Incorporate the almond flour until creamy, then add cream cheese. Continue to mix until the dough shapes, kneading it gently with wet hands if necessary.

2. Break the dough into two parts and stretch out between two parchments to 1/4" thickness. Cut another slice of parchment to match your Power XL Air Fryer tray.

3. Put a piece of flatbread on your parchment and in the Air Fryer and work in two lots if necessary.

4. Select bake mode the set the temperature to 320° F, and set the timer for 7 minutes.

5. Turn the flat-bread halfway through the cooking time. Serve hot.

Radish Chips

Ready in about 15 min | Servings 4 | Easy

Ingredients:

- 2 cups of water
- 1-pound of radishes
- 1/4 teaspoon of onion powder
- 1/4 teaspoon of paprika
- 1/2 teaspoon of garlic powder
- 2 tablespoons of coconut oil, melted

Directions:

1. Put water in a medium saucepan over a stovetop and bring to a boil.
2. Cut the top and bottom of each radish, then slice each radish thinly and evenly with a mandolin. For this stage, you might also be using the slicing blade in the food processor.
3. Place the slices of radish in boiling water for 5 minutes, or until they are translucent. Remove from the bath and put in a clean kitchen towel to absorb extra humidity.
4. Put in a big bowl the radish chips with the remaining one's ingredients and seasoning until thoroughly covered in grease. Place radish chips inside the basket of the Power XL Air Fryer.
5. Change to 320° F and set the timer for 5 minutes.
6. Shake a basket during the cooking process, two to three times. Enjoy!

Calzone

Ready in about 30 min | Servings 4 | Normal

Ingredients:

- 1 ½ cups of shredded mozzarella cheese
- ½ cup of blanched finely ground almond flour
- 1 ounce of full-Fat: cream cheese
- 1 large whole egg
- 4 large eggs, scrambled
- ½ pound cooked breakfast sausage, crumbled
- 8 tablespoons of shredded mild Cheddar cheese

Directions:

1. In a large microwave-safe bowl, add mozzarella, almond flour, and cream cheese—microwave for 1 minute. Stir until the mixture is smooth and forms a ball. Add the egg and stir until dough forms.
2. Place dough between two sheets of parchment and roll out to ¼ " thickness. Cut the dough into four rectangles.
3. Mix scrambled eggs and cooked sausage together ina large bowl. Divide the mixture evenly among each dough piece, placing it on the lower half of the rectangle. Sprinkle each with 2 tablespoons Cheddar.
4. Fold over the rectangle to cover the egg and meat mixture. Pinch, roll, or use a wet fork to close the edges completely.
5. Cut a parchment piece to fit your Power XL Air Fryer basketand place the calzones onto the parchment. Place parchment into the Air Fryer basket.
6. Adjust the temperature to 380° F and set the timer for 15 minutes.
7. Flip the calzones halfway through the cooking time. When done, calzones should be golden in color. Serve immediately.

Enjoy!

Hash Brown Toast

Ready in about 17 min | Serves 4 | Normal

Ingredients:

- 4 hash brown patties, frozen
- 1 tablespoon olive oil
- ¼ cup cherry tomatoes, chopped
- 3 tablespoons mozzarella cheese, shredded
- 2 tablespoons Parmesan cheese, grated
- 1 tablespoon balsamic vinegar
- 1 tablespoon basil, chopped

Directions:

1. Place hash brown patties in your Power XL Air Fryer, pour oil over them and cook at 400° F for 7 minutes.
2. In a bowl, mix tomatoes with mozzarella, parmesan, vinegar and basil and toss well.
3. Divide hash brown patties among plates, top each with tomato mixture and serve for lunch.

Enjoy.

Roasted Garlic

Ready in about 20 min | Servings 1 | Easy

Ingredients:
- 1 medium head of garlic
- 2 teaspoons of avocado oil

Directions:

1. Strip any excess peel hanging from the garlic still cover the cloves. Shutdown 1/4 of the garlic handle, with clove tips visible.

2. Avocado oil spray. Place the garlic head in a small sheet of aluminum foil, and enclose it completely. Place it in the basket for Power XL Air Fryer.

3. Set the temperature to 400° F and change the timer for 20 minutes. If your garlic head is a little smaller, take 15 minutes to check it out.

4. Ail should be golden brown and very fluffy when finished.

5. Cloves should pop out to eat and be scattered or sliced quickly. In the refrigerator, lock in an airtight jar for up to 5 days. You can also freeze individual cloves on a baking sheet, then lock them together until frozen in a freezer-safe storage jar.

Spicy Cheese Meatballs

Ready about in: 15 min|Serves 4|Easy

Ingredients

- 600g Cheddar cheese in cubes
- 240g Clean Chilies
- 2 eggs beaten with salt
- Doritos
- Olive oil

Directions:

In a processor, add half of the Chilies and cheese until you have a paste.

Cut the rest of the chilies finely and incorporate them into the dough. Knead until integrating all the chilies. Grind the Doritos to make a powder. Assemble the meatballs.

Pass them by egg and Doritos. Brush them with olive oil and add them to the Power XL Air Fryer.

Fry at 360° F for 5 to 8 minutes.

When the timer reaches 0, then press the cancel button

Serve up with yogurt sauce, alone or with pink sauce

Egg & Bacon Sandwich

- Ready in about 12 min | Servings 1 | Easy
- Ingredients:
- 2 Bacon Slices
- 1 Egg
- 1 English muffin
- Salt and pepper to the taste

Directions:

1. Beat the egg into asoufflé cup and add salt and pepper to taste.

2 Select bake mode the set the temperature to Power XL Air Fryer to 390°F and place the soufflé cup, English muffin, and bacon into the tray.

3. When the timer reaches 0, then press the cancel button

4. Cook all the ingredients for 6-10 minutes.

Assemble the sandwich and Enjoy!

Ricotta Wraps & Spring Chicken

Ready about in 20 min| Servings: 12

Ingredients

- 2 large-sized chicken breasts, cooked and shredded
- ⅓ tablespoons sea salt
- ¼ tablespoons ground black pepper, or more to taste
- 2 spring onions, chopped
- ¼ cup soy sauce
- 1 tablespoons molasses
- 1 tablespoons rice vinegar
- 10 ounces Ricotta cheese
- 1 tablespoons grated fresh ginger
- 50 wonton wrappers

Directions:

In a bowl, combine all of the ingredients, minus the wonton wrappers.

Unroll the wrappers and spritz with cooking spray.

Fill each of the wonton wrappers with equal amounts of the mixture.

Dampen the edges with a little water as an adhesive and roll up the wrappers, fully enclosing the filling.

Cook the rolls in the Poweer XL Air Fryer for 5 minutes at 375°F. You will need to do this step in batches.

Serve with your preferred sauce.

Chicken Wrapped in Bacon

Ready about in : 25 min | Servings: 6 |

Ingredients

- 6 rashers unsmoked back bacon
- 1 small chicken breast
- 1 tablespoons garlic soft cheese

Directions:

Cut the chicken breast into six bite-sized pieces.

Spread the soft cheese across one side of each slice of bacon.

Put the chicken on top of the cheese and wrap the bacon around it, holding it in place with a toothpick.

Transfer the wrapped chicken pieces to the Power XL Air Fryer and cook for 15 minutes at 350°F.

When the timer reaches 0, then press the cancel button

Veal Club Sandwich

Ready in about 30 min | Servings 2 | Normal

Ingredients:

- 2 slices of white bread
- 1 tablespoons of softened butter
- ½ libbre of cubed veal
- 1 small capsicum
- <u>For Barbeque Sauce:</u>
- ¼ tablespoons of Worcestershire sauce
- ½ tablespoons of olive oil
- ½ flake garlic crushed
- ¼ cup of chopped onion
- ¼ tablespoons of mustard powder
- ½ tablespoons of sugar
- ¼ tablespoons of red chili sauce

Directions:

1. Take the bread slices and cut the rims. Still cut horizontally on the strips. Heat the sauce ingredients and wait before sauce thickens. Now apply the veal to the sauce, and whisk until the flavors are obtained.
2. Whisk the capsicum and scrape off the flesh. The capsicum is sliced into strips. Mix the ingredients, and add them to the slices of bread.
3. Select bake mode the set the temperature to preheat the Power XL Air Fryer to 300° F for 5 minutes. Open the Fryer's basket and put the cooked sandwiches in it, ensuring that no two sandwiches meet each other.

4. Hold the Air Fryer at about 15 minutes now at 250° F. Switch the sandwiches to cook both slices in between the cooking process. Serve the strawberry ketchup or mint chutney sandwiches.

5. Enjoy

Pork Club Sandwich

Ready in about 30 min | Servings 2 | Normal

Ingredients:

- 2 slices of white bread
- 1 tablespoons of softened butter
- ½ lb. of cut pork (get the meat cut into cubes)
- 1 small capsicum
- <u>For Barbeque Sauce:</u>
- ¼ tablespoons of Worcestershire sauce
- ½ tablespoons of olive oil
- ½ flake garlic crushed
- ¼ cup chopped onion
- ¼ tablespoons of mustard powder
- ½ tablespoons of sugar
- ¼ tablespoons of red chili sauce
- 1 tablespoons of tomato ketchup
- ½ cup of water.
- A pinch of salt and black pepper to the taste

Directions:

1. Take the bread slices and cut the rims. Still cut horizontally on the strips. Heat the sauce ingredients and wait before the sauce thickens. Now apply the pork to the sauce and whisk before the flavors are acquired.

2. Whisk the capsicum and scrape off the flesh. The capsicum is sliced into strips. Mix the ingredients, and add them to the slices of bread.

3. Select bake mode the set the temperature to preheat the Power XL Air Fryer to 300° F for 5 minutes.

3. Open the Fryer's basket and put the cooked sandwiches in it, ensuring that no two sandwiches meet each other. Hold the fryer at about 15 minutes now at 250°.

4. Switch the sandwiches to cook both slices in between the cooking process. Serve the strawberry ketchup or mint chutney sandwiches.

Nutrition: Calories: 377 kcal.

Parmesan Herb Focaccia

Ready in about 20 min | Servings 6 | Normal

Ingredients:

- 1 cup of shredded mozzarella cheese
- 1 ounce of full-Fat: cream cheese
- 1 cup of blanched finely ground almond flour
- 1/4 cup of ground golden flaxseed
- 1/4 cup of grated Parmesan cheese
- 1/2 teaspoon of baking soda
- 2 large eggs
- 1/2 teaspoon of garlic powder
- 1/4 teaspoon of dried basil
- 1/4 teaspoon of dried rosemary
- 2 tablespoons of salted butter, melted and divided

Directions:

1. In a large microwave-safe bowl and microwave, put the mozzarella, cream cheese, and almond flour for 1 minute. Add parmesan, flaxseed, and baking soda, and swirl until the ball becomes flat. If the mixture cools too soon, so blending is going to be difficult. Return to the microwave to rewarm for 10–15 seconds if required.

2. Substitute chickens. You may need to use your hands to integrate them to the full. Only keep cooking, and incorporate them into the batter.

3. Mix the garlic powdered dough with the basil and rosemary and knead into the dough. Grease 1 tablespoon melted butter into a round baking pan. Place the dough in the pan equally. Put the pan in the basket for the Power XL Air Fryer.

4. Select bake mode the set the temperature to 400° F and change the timer for 10 minutes.

5. Cover with foil at 7 minutes if the bread starts getting too dark.

6. Remove and cool for at least 30 minutes, mix with remaining butter and serve.

Jicama Fries

Ready in about 30 min | Servings 4 | Easy

Ingredients:

- 1 small jicama, peeled
- 3/4 teaspoon of chili powder
- 1/4 teaspoon of garlic powder
- 1/4 teaspoon of onion powder
- 1/4 teaspoon of ground black pepper

Directions:

1. Break the jicama into 1" cubes. Put in a wide bowl and mix with the coconut oil until seasoned. Sprinkle with the pepper and salt. Put the pepper and onion in the Power XL Air Fryer container.

2. Change the temperature to 400° F and set a 10-minute timer.

3. When the timer reaches 0, then press the cancel button

4. When frying, shake two to three times. Jicama will be soft and dark around the edges and serve immediately.

Fried Green Tomatoes

Ready in about 17 min | Servings 4 | Easy

Ingredients:
- 2 medium green tomatoes
- 1 large egg
- 1/4 cup of blanched finely ground almond flour
- 1/3 cup of grated Parmesan cheese

Directions:

1. Slice the tomatoes into 1/2" thick strips. Whisk the egg in a medium bowl. Mix the almond flour and Parmesan in a big bowl.

2. Dip each slice of tomato into the egg, then dredge in the mixture of almond flour, and put the slices in the Power XL Air Fryer basket.

3. Select bake mode the set the temperature to 400° F, and set the timer for 7 minutes.

4. When the timer reaches 0, then press the cancel button

5. Turn the slices halfway through the duration of preparation. Serve immediately.

Cauliflower Relish

Ready in about 22 min | Servings 4 | Easy

Ingredients:

- 1 head of cauliflower, cut into small florets
- 2 teaspoons of garlic powder
- 1 tablespoon of butter, melted
- 1/2 cup of chili sauce
- Olive oil
- Pinch salt and pepper

Directions:

1. In a bowl, pour oil over cauliflower florets to lightly cover—season with salt, pepper, and garlic powder and toss.
2. Place into Power XL AirFryer at 350°F for 14 minutes and remove. Add together thechili sauce and melted butter, then pour over the florets to coat well.
3. Return to the AirFryer and cook for 3 to 4 minutes longer.
Enjoy!

Baked Zucchini Fries

Ready in about 22 min | Servings 4 | Easy

Ingredients:

- 3 medium zucchinis, sliced lengthwise
- 1/2 cup of seasoned breadcrumbs
- 2 egg, the white part
- 1/4 teaspoon of garlic powder
- 2 tablespoons of parmesan cheese, grated
- Salt and pepper to taste

Directions

1. Beat egg whites in a bowl and season with salt and pepper.
2. In a separate bowl, combine garlic powder, breadcrumbs, and cheese.
3. Dip the zucchini sticks into the egg, bread crumb, and cheese mixture one after the other, then place on a single layer in the Power XL Air Fryer tray.
4. Coat lightly with cooking spray and bake for about 15 minutes at 390°F until golden brown.
5. Serve with a marinara sauce for dipping.

Homemade Tater Tots

Ready in about 30 min | Servings 2 | Easy

Ingredients:

- 1 medium-sized russet potato, chopped
- 1 teaspoon of ground onion
- 1 teaspoon of vegetable oil
- ½ teaspoon of ground black pepper
- Salt to taste

Directions:

1. Boil the potatoes until a bit more than al dente. Drain off water, add onions, oil, and pepper to it, and mash.
2. Select bake mode the set the temperature to preheat the Power XL Air Fryer to 379°F.
3. Mold the mash potatoes into tater tots. Place into the AirFryer and bake for8 minutes. Shake the tots and bake for 5 minutes longer.

PUBLISHIG HOUSE
KULTURE KITCHEN

www.ingramcontent.com/pod-product-compliance
Lightning Source LLC
Chambersburg PA
CBHW070939080526
44589CB00013B/1567